mini manifester

Abigail Simmonds

Illustrated by Bryony Fripp

Published by
Hasmark Publishing
www.hasmarkpublishing.com

Disclaimer:
This book is designed to provide information and motivation to our readers. It is sold with the understanding that the publisher is not engaged to render any type of psychological, legal, or any other kind of professional advice. The content of each article is the sole expression and opinion of its author, and not necessarily that of the publisher. No warranties or guarantees are expressed or implied by the publisher's choice to include any of the content in this volume. Neither the publisher nor the individual author(s) shall be liable for any physical, psychological, emotional, financial, or commercial damages, including, but not limited to, special, incidental, consequential or other damages. Our views and rights are the same: You are responsible for your own choices, actions, and results.

Permission should be addressed in writing to Abigail Simmonds at abigail@minimanifester.com

Illustrator: Bryony Fripp www.bryonyfripp.com

Editor: Jamie Geidel jamie@hasmarkpublishing.com

Cover Designer: Anne Karklins anne@hasmarkpublishing.com

Layout Artist: Amit Dey amit@hasmarkpublishing.com

ISBN 13: 978-1-77482-198-5

ISBN 10: 1774821982

For Isabella, Francesco, and Rosalia.

Always trust the magic of your imagination.

I have been searching for a book just like this for my young daughters, to help introduce the concept of manifestation to them in a way they can understand! *Mini Manifester* is beautifully written and illustrated, my girls love reading it. I especially love the affirmations at the end to help them begin to build a belief in themselves that they are enough, and that they are capable of achieving all of their dreams! Thank you for creating such a beautiful and inspiring book for our youth!
Elizabeth Plancon, International Bestselling Author of *Manifesting With Purpose*

Mini Manifester is beautifully written and illustrated. The rhymes are engaging, and the colourful illustrations are inspiring to children. Above all, the messages will give them a foundation of confidence and self-esteem.
— **Judy O'Beirn,** International Bestselling Author

Mini Manifester is an adorable and happy little book that will inspire and uplift a young heart. The illustrations are beautifully done, and the message is a powerful one.
— **Peggy McColl,** *New York Times Best Selling Author*

I wake up early, I'm still yawning,

but it's time to start my morning.

I know if I want to be my best

there are ways to help me manifest.

I have so many goals and dreams,

I must take action to make them real.

I think about how I feel today

and repeat to myself that I am safe.

I allow myself to feel any way

and accept there are things I can not change.

The best way to lift my mood

is to write a list of gratitude.

I drink my water and write my list,

I'm so grateful, life's a gift.

I stretch my body and exercise,

and now it's time to visualize.

I look at my vision board and feel clear,

I never give up, I never fear.

I sit and listen to my breath,

a daily reminder to love myself.

I imagine the places I will go,

what I'll do, and what I'll show.

I know I'm attracting positivity

because I have high energy.

I expect my dreams and goals to come true,

I feel the joy because they always do.

I think and live as though it's mine,

I know it's just a matter of time,

and when I go to bed at night

I keep the vision, I don't lose sight.

I am peaceful

I am beautiful

I am grateful

I am happy

I am kind

I am important

I am enough

I am confident

I am loved

I tell myself what I've known all along that

I am brilliant and I am strong.

I am brave and kind to all,

I am confident, I stand tall.

So now I truly do believe

that anything I can achieve,

Because everything I want to be

is already *here* inside of me.

Abigail Simmonds lives in the UK with her family; she is a mum to Francesco and Rosalia and step-mum to Isabella. Abigail has a great interest in manifestation and the strong connection between the power of the mind and how we create in the physical world, which she believes should be taught from a young age.

Mini Manifester is Abigail's first book and was created to inspire children to follow their dreams and believe in themselves with the help of daily habits such as affirmations and meditation, and the wonder of imagination.

For More Information about Abigail Simmonds

@ABIGAILSIMMONDS
@MINIMANIFESTER

ABIGAIL@MINIMANIFESTER.COM

Where to Buy the Book

WWW.MINIMANIFESTER.COM

Hearts to be Heard

Giving a Voice to Creativity!

From: Circe'

To: Kids who love to write stories!

How would you like to have your story in a book? A real book!
Hearts to be Heard will make that happen.

Get started now at
HeartstobeHeard.com

Also visit HH Kid's Corner for creative writing activities!
HeartstobeHeard.com/kids-corner/

Printed in Great Britain
by Amazon

26490292R00023